Enjoy daddy
and his bulge

sexy

/ˈsɛksi/

adjective

    1. 1.

  sexually attractive or exciting.

  "sexy French underwear"

synonyms:

sexually attractive, seductive, desirable, alluring, inviting,
sensual, sultry, slinky, provocative, tempting, tantalizing;
More

    1. 2.

  INFORMAL

  very exciting or appealing.

  "business magazines might not seem like the sexiest
  career choice"

synonyms:

exciting, stimulating, interesting, appealing, intriguing;

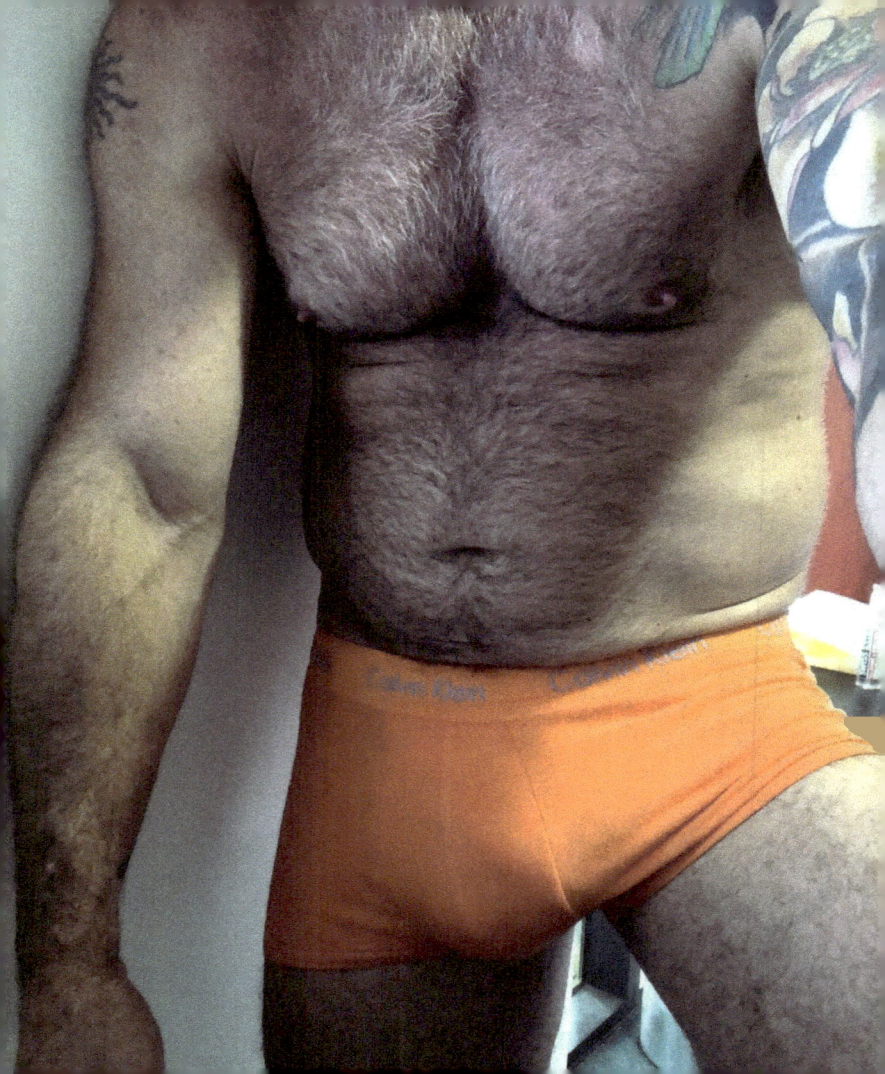

CPSIA information can be obtained
at www.ICGtesting.com
Printed in the USA
BVHW090824010419
544230BV00037B/1997/P

9 780368 500879